The Abelard Poets

IN THE GLASS OF WINTER

The Abelard Poets

IN THE GLASS OF WINTER

DAVID JAFFIN

With an Introduction by Edward Lucie-Smith

Abelard-Schuman · London

For my parents

First published 1975
ISBN 0 200 72280 8

Abelard-Schuman Limited *450 Edgware Road, London W2*
and *Kingswood House, Heath and Reach, Leighton Buzzard, Bedfordshire*
Printed in Great Britain
by Billing & Sons Limited, Guildford and London

Contents

These poems have appeared in the following periodicals:

The Contemporary Review; English (Oxford University Press); Tribune; The Dublin Magazine (Ireland); The Chelsea Review (USA); Ariel (University of Calgary, Canada); The Christian Century (USA); Meridian Poetry Magazine; The Decal Review; Workshop New Poetry; The Anglo Welsh Review; The Antigonish Review (St. Francis Xavier University, Canada); Tagus; Samphire; In Dark Mill Shadows (Anthology of Bailrigg Poems, University of Lancaster); Poet (London); The Dalhousie Review (Dalhousie University, Canada); The Little Word Machine; The Literary Half Yearly (University of Mysore, India); Littack; Capella (Ireland); The Chapman; The Clare Market Review (London School of Economics); The Wisconsin Review (USA); Poem (USA); The Galley Sail Review (USA); The Wascana Review (University of Saskatchewan, Canada); The Roanoke Review (Roanoke College, USA); The University of Portland Review (USA); Gallery Series Poets (USA); The Florida Quarterly (University of Florida, USA); Waves (University of York, Canada); The Washington and Jefferson Literary Journal (Washington and Jefferson College, USA); Orbis; The Free Lance (USA); Here Now; Gong (University of Nottingham); The Whetstone (USA); Platform (Yorkshire); Muse (Birmingham Poetry Centre).

Introduction

It is a matter for concern, as well as for curiosity, that the struggle to be modern has had, in the English language at least, such an intermittent success. Much consciously 'modernist' poetry written in English is forced and pretentious; but work which shuns experiment is often pretentious and boring. Things are different abroad. In France, the ethos of the Modern Movement permeates contemporary poetry as much as it does painting and sculpture, and developments in poetry have been inseparably linked with those which have taken place in the visual arts. Expressionist painting in Germany ran parallel with the development of Expressionism in literature, and especially in poetry; and the modernist development which Hitler checked has been taken up again with renewed vigour in the years since 1945, as we can see in the works of poets otherwise as different from one another as Enzensberger and Celan. In the literature of Spain and of the Spanish-speaking Americas the vitality of the poets—they range from the vigour of Neruda to the severity of Nicanor Parra—has perhaps surpassed that of the visual artists produced by the same group of cultures.

It will take many writers, not just one writer, to remedy this situation where English is concerned, but David Jaffin is certainly one of the few who seem to be aware of the problem. His poems are brief, and at a first reading look very simple. It is only as we re-read them that we realize how subtly he handles his linguistic material. Many of his most characteristic effects come from small but nevertheless vitally important displacements of words—from their usual function or their usual context. Here are some examples, chosen almost at random: 'Memory *lights* the scent/of lilac'—'When winter comes/We take a book *to ourselves*/From those long *covered* shelves/of silence'—'You touched/Your fingers *placed silence/in place*'.

This sensitivity to the weight and meanings of words, and the way in which the meaning can be altered by a number of different factors: context, grammatical function, position in the line, the overall rhythm of the poem—here is something which makes it clear that David Jaffin has nothing to do with 'academic poetry' of a conventionally skilful kind.

One reason why we read poems is because they refresh the language, because they bring words alive, and rub off the tarnish which accumulates in daily usage. This cleansing function is one of the most important the poet can exercise, though it is not necessarily the one which will make his work immediately popular. David Jaffin's characteristic spareness and economy make the reader particularly keenly aware of his concern for good language, which means fresh and immediate language. He deserves to be read because he improves and extends the instrument he uses.

Edward Lucie-Smith

[I] PREFACE

The tentative light of the
  winter dawn,
Its cold truth I break with
  this song;

Incomplete I left the
  flower
Before my lips could form
  its presence.

GREEN SCARF

I am of the winter of
  your eyes:

The mist
  (the flower cold)

You circling on that
  field,

Your green scarf
  (this circled sun),

The sorrow of our love;

Why among the clouds so
  shaped and solemn,

Memory lights the scent
  of lilac?

WHEN WINTER COMES

When winter comes
We close the windows behind us,
Seal off that last bit of cold
  from within us
And consider the warmth inside.

We are rooms then,
With emptied spaces and shutters
  without,
Perfectly planned we stand to
Within the centre of ourselves
And turn that switch between
  light and darkness.

When winter comes
We take a book to ourselves
From those long covered shelves
  of silence
And feel out the pages
  of sound
To our stretched out thoughts
  recede,

Touch to each a quickened vein
At a fire of our own
  asking:
Wine, and the wintered
  winds without.

GETTING OLD

You were getting old they
  told me,
The fires gone from your face,
Burned to the coolness of
  diminished flame,
The heat in being constant,
Coals that kept their purpose
  still;

You were getting old they
  told me,
Hands less quick to grasp
But slow to yield
As if touch could replace that
Active thought of yours—

And yes,
They told me you sat by the
  fire now,
Days on end, not thinking
At all but watching those flames
Diminish to their final
  glow.

UPON A STILL GLASS

Ask in silence me,
The words have whispered
  found

as breath upon a
  still glass

then cease to be.

AT EASE

And that afternoon
We sat at ease, I had waited
Long for your coming,
With hat in hand
And the winds had blown
Whatever thoughts I had,
  away,
Before you came and we took
A loaf of bread between
  us,
Sliced it to the last frag-
  ments of sun

And it was like looking
  in,
You talked and it was
Like looking in a door we'd
Already closed behind
And all those seats were
  filled before,
The faces wanted to be
  away

But you brought them nearer,
Constantly nearer—
Was it your hands,
The quiet intonation of your
  voice?

And they sat
And we sat looking at the
  same thing,
At a word we'd focused on,
And the candle on the table
Standing at the middle
Blew repeatedly upon its
  own flame.

THAT AFTERNOON IN SALZBURG

I sit in the afternoon.
It could be a garden
   here
And the fountains would be on
Turning their clear light
As people pass
Between rows of gardened grass

I sit where I am,
Time and place are all the
Same in this ordered
   scene
I sit and think
Or I come and go between
These rows of conscious
   sounds

Nothing takes place.
People pass, the fountains are
Lit, on, flowers open out
Their face to that all consuming
   sun

But the shadows are gathering
   sounds
The still's become cold
And I've grown conscious of
These stones I'm looking at
And sitting on
The sun sinks, its tendered
Light, a wind without a mark
Quicker now, each time the
Shadows break, people pass as
Birds take flight
                              fainter still
      from here.

WITH A CHANGE IN THE WINDS

Sadness came in the night
With a change in the winds
It left snow,
It left a face of clearness,
It deceived for its own sake.

And in the morning
When we heard the men working
Between the hills,
Sounds that echoed out
And birds that circled there
Self enclosed in shadow

Where the winds crossed as
  waves of sound

Sadness came that night
And we felt it between ourselves,
Distances there that were
Covered over too and deceptively
  clear.

AT NIGHT BY THE FIRE

It is better not to say.
Quietness at least conceals.
It can be touched to
The cloth work turn of
  your hands
At night by the fire
When your face was a pause
  in the shadows
And flames sparkled their
  thirst
We remained to the corners of
That room we called familiar
  once
Concealing ourselves there
From the winds that told
  without
And the flames that burned
  their cause away.

THAT ROOM

There must be quiet
And there must be beauty,
Whichever way the world
goes
Here it stays still,
Here it is brought to and
Here it shall find

As a chair in an empty
room,
Hardly noticed at first
Concealing space where
You sat, you as you
And drawn to within the
Qualities of yourself.

Let us close that door now
To silence and to beauty
And to rest, and let us
Listen in that calmed
stillness
To the voice of our own
concealed voice.

I

The sun is broken,
Its face of glass reflected the
   image I—

Not the I of myself,
But the glass, the image
   reflected.

Fear is of two wings
   (flight but shadow)
That distils this silence, the

   awkward pain—

Fear that these eyes would
   meet themselves

that dream was but fancy,
   of cloth woven

that when I touched your
   hand

It was only the wind,
   and i.

DYING

It was that room again,
The same and ever present and walked
into

As the sea with its life like
Sounds that could have been drawn even
closer once

He stirred, the light
Changed and his eyes were half
expectant

As she came in his mind
Down those corridors of
sound

And he thought of summer then,
The stillness of being loved,
The counting out of things
together, and after

(that light changed)

Not at a moment to be taken
in hand
Or with a switch

He lay in shadow
Conscious of those sheets that
couldn't cool

About him night closed it
self round,
The ringing out of stars
And that bright, apparent
moon

It was that room again,
The same and ever present and
walked into
He prepared, he neared his
own parting.

CLOSED BEHIND

And when we went a bit further
The fence closed behind.
It swang, the way Robert Frost
Wrote of birch swingers,
But it closed. It wasn't our choice.
We didn't even think of it then,
Not till later, the sun had
Climbed over the hill before us
And winter was at its brightest
Despite those shifting shades and
The pastel sky that added a
Tone of lightness to our step
As we passed through the powdered
Snow and noticed row upon row
How that fence had widened itself out
Until we were closed within

And when we went a bit further
We came to a wood.
It was light at first,
Combs of birch stood at the sides
But before we realized where we
Were it had darkened,
The trees became higher, the
Snow deeper, the world
Darker, and we couldn't think, not
Even then, of turning back,
We kept going on and on
Deeper and deeper into that closing
Darkness until at once
I lit a flame to my fingers to
Take that cold away
And when I looked you weren't
There and I turned round to where
We'd been before, but
Our steps had blown away.

IN LIGHT

You were alone in a room.
The light lit you
It fell where you were
And folded your hands
    together
Creating a moment

You touched
Your fingers placed silence
    in place
Rethinking sounds
Recollecting thoughts

You closed that door
    quietly, behind
Went out, into the
    sun

Your dress creased
Your mind absorbed light
Your fingers ceased to
    think
For themselves

As you stepped quickly in-
    stead
Aside from what you
    thought

And were gone in a
Moment of shadow and
    shade.

LATE HARVEST

The last fruit is almost in,
The fields will be stubble
        and stone
And what we've forgotten to take,
        dried,

The trees will loose their leaves
As you did for me once,
        your hair,
And that sun will turn cold,
    to touch.

Let us walk now,
Let us take hands, for we are
        less than this.

[II] AT THE GATE

Here, waiting at the gate
The sun slipped quickly through
  my hands
As the scales of a fish
Left shining in light

Steel touched I stood
Where the sky had ceased to
  move in me
Its clustered sounds of
  snow
The stroking of the winds

Trees stepped, footwise
  higher
For the leaves to turn
Their stillness

  out

And the gate,
Prefigured, cold watching
  night.

ENCOUNTERED

That day
Cold and clear as a conscious
   flame

I feared as I fear myself now,
Not knowing how it came to
   this,

Cold and clear
As light that wants itself, a
Brightness without cause you
   came,

Eyes wanton flame,
Nearer to my own than this
That flesh I called
   myself,

Marbled/spoken stone see-
   ing presence there.

19 DAYS

For 19 days
We didn't see the sun

It disappeared over
night we grew closer

to ourselves
in the cold mist

followed our steps
from behind

listening to sound
the touched-presence of

stone

What we couldn't see
we felt, even

if the cold numbed
our hands we went

without hats
that space could be heard

We kept close together
breathing the warmed air

We wanted rooms to be
lit when we came,

identified their space

We stood before mir-
rors hours at

a time looking at
our eyes those 19 days

without sun.

LADDER

That ladder
led its way from
place to place

of former chance,
traced the
cause (barely con-

strued) deci-
phered then,

hands held fast
feet secure

One wanted more
scope toward

the top it
came, that lad-

der led the
same way down.

CITIES

This time we had to pass
walls we couldn't climb

They were preconceived
as an eye that closes
with a switch

They stared through
fountains, hollowed
stillness as a woman

petitions coldness with
the touch of a na-
ked hand

Night descended still
without stars

the moon a foil
to itself.

NEARING SPRING

A man's picture
Taken in the papers, worn
  with the print,

A pipe leaning beside
  on a tray
Pursuing its own aimless
way in that emptied
  room

No one sits there,
A radio could be on
The curtains could be hung
  to appear bright

Perhaps a cat's
Creeping along the roof,
Keeping its paws close
  to its own sounds

And perhaps the rain's been
  turned on
And there's a vacancy of
  light,
A dullness of grass

Nearing spring
I could read it from your
  face,
What's been worn and
Where the print's
  coming loose.

ON HIS ILLNESS

He felt the leaves
   run dry,
In the blue sunlight

He was cold to thought,
The abstractions of
   time

He asked if the flower
   could bleed its

      scent away.

AQUARIUM

They've never thought that way,
Light means nothing to them
only the borders of sound,
The cold rimmed glass

As they run
That flash of steel their
   prismic thoughts
Closed in to the sun of their own
   unconscious selves

Those scales, that
Light means nothing to them
only the borders of sound,
The cold rimmed glass.

STEPS IN SNOW

There were steps there
That led across the snow, clearly,
From this house to the road.

I remember how they looked at first,
The impression that they made of
Distinctness, freshness

That I could almost feel the
Boots meet that crush of snow and
The clear impressions they

Left, after. And
Then it froze, winter sank to
Its deepest point and

Those steps hardened then,
Without person, intombed in a
Certain stillness as the

Mark of a previous age.
And now it's melting, that path
Itself is thawing and it

No longer meets the road,
And it doesn't quite start from
The house, and at times
Between it can't really find
Its own way out.

IN THE GLASS OF WINTER

He had never heard himself.

Everything has sound he
thought, the trees

need wind the clouds
snow but they can be

heard.

When he was 8
he saw himself once

in a mirror
imagined his death

Eyes can't see them-
selves without glass

He knew he'd put this
edge to himself

It took 4 years
before he began to listen

usually in the rain

if he heard hard enough
and saw shadows

He thought he'd felt
    himself

but once a bird passed
and he knew he was

    gone

Or if he listened
long enough

there was only rain

But now
at 36 he's stopped

listening

he's put the shades
where he wants

but at night
every once in a while

He looks at the moon
touches the dark

and's afraid.

AGING

The day closed as a curtain
folded at either end

certain to meet at the
      middle—

Winds waste away
      out there

You found the light and
combed your hair,

pursued thoughts that
      weren't there;

Time recedes, as
      touch

You felt very much
      that way

(without feeling at all)

Except the bright of
      day

closed as a curtain
folded at either

      end.

MISCONCEIVED

As we sat by the fire,
Preserved the winter's flame

I touched your hand
observed the same

Forgot precisely the ad-
equate name for such

    feelings;

Presumed the presence of
    flowers

assumed it was May,
But you, my dear

    exclaimed
That's a long time

    away.

ESTABLISHED

Can you imagine her now
With children steeped from head to
    toe
In a flowing gown and
All that regalia of justice,

She who spat upon her mother's knee,
Who taught her masters oft
A lesson or two,
Extended her tongue (when she was
still quite young) between
The upper teeth and the garlicked
Dungeons of her lower mouth?

Can you imagine her now
Treading the church with a drawn down
    brow
And all the appearance of a somewhat
    contemplation
When she used to kick between the chairs
And mimic the worthy airs of an
    elder generation?

Can you think of her as stately
And fine, jewelled and gowned
In the prismic order of
    the present?

ALL BEFORE

She had danced it all before.
Swung softly to the
    right
Hips swayed, asked casually
If you liked the featured
    parts,
The prettied portions of her
Face appearing on the
    family page

At length she crossed
    her legs,
Adjusted the smile
Paused awhile raising that
    glass
To those turned up
lips flittered away among
    the guests.

BALLROOM SCENE (AFTER FRANCESCO DE GUARDI)

The world's turned cold,
Naked for the mind
And the eye to be-

hold its solitary light

As truth once told,
disenchanted;

Touch defined,
Crystalled light the
Mind as glass

To its cause, insuf-
ficiently.

BRIDGE

The winds are sharp,
The waters cut with a
   blade

The sky should be steel
   blue

Whatever I touch shines
   cold in my hands

Thoughts edged in glass
The mirrored frame of
   fear

This cold glistens its
Sound and the waves are moved
   by swans

Tucked in their wings
As persons closed in the folds of
   their coats

A bridge crosses the water
   from either side
Steps that can't be heard

We've told to ourselves
And don't lead as sounds,
   to.

ON A WEDNESDAY AFTERNOON

Somewhere he's sitting and thinking
himself out

on a park bench

beneath barren trees
and self accustomed stones

on a Wednesday afternoon.

He hears the sounds of his
own thoughts

He's listening closely.

Shadows blow in the wind
quickly

His hand touches wood.

He's trying to stand
now

Children jump squares be-
side him

A fountain should be on
but isn't

He turns now and's going
home.

VACANCIES OF SOUND

This room is dying in
    my heat
The sun draws its flames
    from me

Flowers stain
that I cut with my bare
    hands

in the window's light

As a fire rubbed to the
quick of its own

    thirst

The colours run
Into pools of stagnant
    streams

I close the windows for my
eyes to look out of

    nothing within
except the vacancies of
    sound

The city held from its
breath as a wind with
    out touch

I sleep the final sleep
    of death.